Book Of Poems

T.C. Shadowbrook

BookLeaf
Publishing

India | USA | UK

Made with ❤ on the BookLeaf Publishing Platform

www.bookleafpub.in

www.bookleafpub.com

Dedication

For the reader—
Thank you for opening these pages and sharing in the
journey. Your quiet support gives these words meaning.
May you find something of yourself in these lines, and
know you are appreciated, even if we never meet.

Preface

These poems were written in quiet moments, collected over untold days. They come from places both gentle and restless, meant to be discovered by whoever needs them. I offer these words, hoping they bring a little light or comfort, wherever they land.

Acknowledgements

Grateful to the unseen hands, gentle voices, and passing days that shaped these pages. The names are many, and none need to be spoken.

1. Big Picture

When did the world forget to look at the big picture?
We are so focused on the present moment.
It is essential to stop and smell the roses.
It is essential to live in the moment.
But never forget, today's actions do affect tomorrow
We are all pieces in a puzzle,
connected in ways we don't even know.

We must think about the impact of our actions,
not just on ourselves, but on others as well.
We must consider the butterfly effect,
how each flap of a wing can cause a storm.

Our world is fragile,
and yet, we treat it like we have another one to spare.
We must widen our view,
look beyond our own needs and wants.

The big picture is complex,
but we cannot afford to ignore it.
We must be mindful of our choices
and remember that they ripple into the future.

The big picture is not always pretty.

But we must face it with courage.
We must take responsibility
for the role we play in this world.

So let's take a step back
and look at the big picture.
Let's work together
to create a better tomorrow.

For in the end,
it's all about the big picture.
So let's paint it with care
and make it a masterpiece.

2. The Cracks in our Love

What should love look like?
When should we love ourselves?
When should we change?
When should we stay who we are?

Broken-hearted because I didn't know what to do.

I didn't know when to change.
I didn't know when to stay the same.
But I knew that I loved you.
And I thought that it was enough
Until it wasn't.

Until the cracks in our love couldn't be ignored
Until we both realized we had changed
But not together
Not in a way that could sustain us
So we fell apart

Broken-hearted, but still in love
With the person we used to be
With the person we hoped we could still be
But love isn't enough

It takes work and compromise.
And sometimes, despite our best efforts,
It still shatters.
Leaving us broken-hearted.
But with the hope that we can piece ourselves back
together.

And maybe, one day, find love again.

3. Echoes of Solitude

Every decision, right or wrong, is on me.
Every fight, when do I get the chance to breathe?
I'm alone, with no support, no friends, and no one who understands.
It is me against the world for my child.
It is me against my child.
Choose your battles.

Every child is different, every problem is unique.
When I'm lost in those moments, it is a lonely ship.
I am the captain, the crew, and the passengers.
I am adrift, in a fog, waiting for a lighthouse that never shines.
I always hope for a peaceful harbor, but it never comes.

The storm rages on, battering my soul, chipping away at my quiet resolve.
I am exhausted in every way, yet I continue to fight the battles, challenge the norm, and be his most significant support.
I want to hand off the wheel, to rest, to laugh, to be carefree.
But that is not my fate, not my reality.

I am a mother, a warrior, a survivor.

And so I continue, in this lonely boat, fighting the waves.

I continue to do my best.

I continue to make decisions.

Will I ever know if it was right?

Will I ever know my best was good enough?

Will I ever know if I choose the right battles?

4. Invisible

Will you see me?
You look right through me.
You see right past me.
You see what's beyond me.
You see the world.
I am a window.

Invisible.

Will you hear me?
My words fall on deaf ears,
I scream until my voice is hoarse
My throat is raw
I keep trying to reach you.

Invisible.

My tears fall on unseeing eyes.
I am the wind, felt but not seen.
I am the night, dark and empty.
The pain, the agony, I am not here.

Invisible.

I am the window.
I am the wind.
I am the night.
I am in pain.
I am invisible.

5. The Art of Growing Up

Working three jobs
paying bills
maintaining a house
raising kids
being a good spouse
and still having time for friends

The expectations of society
are high indeed
And we all want to succeed
But what is success?
Money? Fame? Fortune?
Or is it something more?
Or is it something less?

We are told to grow up
to be responsible adults.
But what does that really mean?
Is it paying taxes on time?
Or remembering to floss every night?

Or is it something deeper?
Something more profound?
Like knowing when to speak up.

When to keep quiet.
When to take a stand.
Or when to let things go?

Is it knowing who we are?
Or what do we want?
And not being afraid
To chase after our dreams?

Or is it simply surviving
in a world that can be not kind?
And standing tall
even when we feel small?

Perhaps it's all these things
and more.
The art of growing up
is an ever-evolving door
that we must continuously open
and explore.

6. Slow and Steady

Buy a house.
Buy a car.
Have savings.
Kids...
Do we have to?
No, we don't.
But that's what you're supposed to do?
Supposed to do?

What if we...
Take our time?
Take it easy?
Don't rush.
Go at our own pace?

Find the right house.
The right car.
Save up for a future we want.
Are kids in the picture?
We'll see.

Why rush through life?
When can we take it slow?
Savor every moment

And enjoy the ride

Slow and steady
Wins the race
But is it really a race
Or just society's expectations?

Let's break free...
From the mold.
And live life.
At our own pace.

7. Suitcases

How does one let go?

Let go, like letting go of a pen?
Let go, like letting a child go to college?
Let go, like burying our loved ones?
Let go, like the dying man breathes his last?

How does one let go of the hurt,
the pain, the anger, the disappointment?
Can it all be neatly packed into suitcases
and carried around like a nomad?

How does one unzip those suitcases
and release their contents into the wind?
How do we trust that the wind will carry them away,
far from our reach, to be buried in the sea,
lost in the mountains, or forgotten in the desert?

How do we stop ourselves from zipping them back in
time and time again?
How do we stop ourselves from putting them in a closet
or storage space to hold onto them?
How do we stop ourselves from keeping it unsafely
stowed away?

How do we stop ourselves from carrying them...
To every new place we go?
To every new relationship we enter?
To every new day we wake up to?

How do we let go, truly, completely,
of all the baggage that weighs us down,
that keeps us from soaring,
that stops us from living in the moment?

How do we let go of the past,
and embrace the unknown future,
with open arms and open hearts?

How do we let go?

8. The Mask of Projection

Innocent until proven guilty?
Does this apply to everyone?
Angry even when the fault is our own.

Misleading others instead of admitting guilt.
Assuming the worst in the other.
Never giving them a chance to explain.

Blaming others for our own mistakes.
Hating them without a reason.
Hurting innocent people with our words.

Judging others harshly.
Projecting our own insecurities.
The mask of projection, the sign of insecurity.

9. A Heart on Fire

My feelings are deep.
My feelings are raw.
But...

I have to hide my feelings.
I have to change who I am for the world's comfort.
My heart is a wildfire that burns inside my chest.
But...

I must smother the flames, lest they consume me.
I am told to be less.
I am told to be quiet.
I am told to be "normal."
But...

I am not normal.
I am not quiet.
I am not less.

I am emotional.
I am passionate.
I am alive.

And that is more than enough.

10. The Mountain

Giving up and trying something different is a strength.
Giving in and learning from someone else is a strength.
Choosing to give our hearts to another is a strength.
Choosing to go it alone is a strength.

Facing our fears is a strength.
Fighting for what we believe in is strength.
Letting go of those we love is a sign of strength.
Holding on to hope is strength.

Opening our hearts to forgiveness is strength.
Closing ourselves off to pain is strength.
Saying goodbye is a strength.
Leaving behind what no longer serves us is a form of
strength.

Embracing new beginnings is a strength.
Being true to ourselves is a strength.
Living with our mistakes is a strength.
Letting the past be the past is a strength.

Looking toward the future is a strength.
Embracing our imperfections is a strength.
Finding beauty in the chaos is a strength.

Believing in ourselves is a strength.

Having faith in something greater is strength.
Standing up for what is right is a strength.
Falling and getting back up are strengths.
Knowing when to say no is a strength.

Knowing when to say yes is a strength.
Being vulnerable is a strength.
Being strong is strength.

We are mountains, unyielding,
But also fragile, with hidden depths.
We must be both to withstand the test of time.

11. Sweet Nothings

When did being honest become the wrong thing to do?
Why must we walk on eggshells to please?
Sugarcoat our words, passive-aggressive.
In our delivery, we are afraid to speak our truth.
For fear of hurting someone's delicate feelings.
But what about our own?

Why must we constantly compromise
our own thoughts and beliefs?

We tiptoe around the truth,
afraid to offend or upset.
But in the end, we are only lying to ourselves.
We must learn to speak our minds,
without fear of repercussion,
and not be afraid to hear the harsh truth
from others as well.

For in the end, honesty is the purest form of love,
And nothing sweet can come from a sugarcoated lie.

12. The Backstabber's Lament

You make me your villain to get your way.
You make me the villain to make you look better.
You make me the villain to hide your own flaws.

I'm not saying I'm perfect; I have my own flaws.
I don't feel the need to make you look bad.
But you do.

You manipulate and twist the truth,
To make me look like the bad guy.
It's a game to you,
And you always win.

Well, I'm done playing.
I refuse to be your pawn any longer.
I won't suck up to you,
Or kiss your ass behind your back.

I won't stab you in the back.
But I also won't let you stab me anymore.
I'll stand up for myself,
And call you out on your lies.

I'll be the villain you want me to be,
Because that's the only way you know how to see me.
But I'll also be true to myself,
And won't let you bring me down.
So go ahead, spread your lies.

I'll be here, standing tall,
With my head held high,
Knowing who I am,
And not letting you change that.

13. Growing Strong

We protect our young, but we hurt them.
Teach them the power of yet.
Teach them the concept of failure.
Teach them that making a mistake is okay.
Teach them that it is essential to learn from these.
Teach them to have grit.
To never give up.
Teach them a growth mindset.
So they can grow strong.

We used to think intelligence is fixed.
But we know better now.
We know that the brain can grow and change.
We know that effort and determination are key.
We know that challenges make us smarter.
We know that failure is not permanent.
We know that we can continually improve.

So let's teach our children this truth.
That their potential is limitless.
That they have the power to change and grow.
Grades or tests do not define their worth.
That they can achieve anything they set their minds to.
That they are capable and resilient.

Let's teach them to embrace challenges.
To see mistakes as opportunities.
To keep trying, even when it's hard.
To believe in themselves.
To have a growth mindset.

So they can grow strong,
And reach for the stars.

14. Constantly Shifting

In life, we are not promised...
...tomorrow.
...good health.
...a decent meal.
...a warm home.
...a chance to speak our truth.
...a lifetime of love.

The things we take for granted,
can be ripped away at a moment's notice.
We are constantly shifting,
changing, evolving,
As the world around us changes, too.

We must learn to adapt,
to bend with the winds of change,
or risk being broken.

The only thing guaranteed is change,
and how we respond to it,
is what truly defines us.

So let us embrace the unknown,
embrace the ever-shifting nature of life,

and find peace in the chaos.

For it is in the midst of change,
that we discover our most authentic selves,
our deepest strengths,
and our most tremendous potential.

Constantly shifting,
We are never the same,
But that is the beauty of life.

15. Puppet Master

He manipulated to get his way.
She manipulates to get her needs met.
Society manipulates to serve the few.
Mankind manipulates to survive.
We all manipulate, in one way or another,
to create the world we desire.

But who is the true puppet master?
Is it the one who pulls the strings,
Or the one who allows themselves to be pulled?

We are all puppets,
dancing to the tune of manipulation.
Sometimes, we are aware of the strings,
and other times, we are blissfully ignorant.

But when we open our eyes,
and see the tangled web of deceit,
We can choose to cut the strings,
and dance to our own beat.

Do not let yourself be controlled
by the sly hands of manipulation.
Take hold of your own strings

and create your own destiny.

The true puppet master is within,
and only you can decide how to wield its power.
So break free from the manipulation
and become the master of your own fate.

16. The Shadow We Leave Behind

We say our past
makes us who we are
makes us stronger

But does it?
I look back on my life.
And see the shadows I've left behind.

The people I've hurt
The hearts I've broken
The lies I've told
The promises I've broken

And I wonder,
Are these shadows my friends or foes?

They remind me of my mistake.s
Of the darkness in my heart
But they also push me to be better
To make amends and move forward

Our past may haunt us.
But it can also guide us.

Reminding us of where we've been
And how far we still have to go

So I embrace my shadows.
As painful as they may be.
For they are a part of me.
And they will always be there.

But I choose to let them be my friends.
My constant reminders
To live with intention
And to never forget the lessons of my past.

For without our shadows
We would not know the beauty of the light

17. The Spark of Creation

Every invention starts at step one.
The creation of fire, the invention of the wheel.
We didn't know what the future would become,
But we knew we had to make that first deal.

A spark ignited from a flint,
Wooden logs are burning bright.
It was the first time we felt warmth,
The first time we saw light.

We felt the power of control,
By the fire's light, we could see,
We could create something from nothing
This was the moment we were set free.

The wheel set us in motion,
And we never looked back.
We could explore and discover,
There was nothing we lacked.

Our imagination ran wild,
As we crafted new tools.
We built homes and weapons,
We weren't just simple fools.

We've come so far since then,
But the spark of creation remains,
We're still driven to invent,
It's a fire that forever flames.

So when you feel lost and low,
When you feel like you can't create,
Remember the spark that started it all,
And let it be your fate.

18. The Persistence of Light

In the darkest of nights, a glimmer of hope
A faint, flickering light that refuses to die
It persists through the storm, through the strife
Guiding us through our darkest moments

It whispers to us in our despair
Whispers of a brighter tomorrow
Whispers of a better world
Whispers that we must hold onto

For even in the depths of our despair
There is always a glimmer of light
A reminder that things will get better
That there is still hope in this world

And so we cling to that light
We hold it close to our hearts
And let it guide us through the darkness
For in the end, it is all we have

So let us never lose hope.
Let us never let that light fade
For it is the only thing that keeps us going
The persistence of light in the darkest of nights.

19. The Burden of Being Human

We are told to be strong, to persevere,
to keep our heads up when others fall,
to march on even when we are tired
and to never give in, no matter what.
We are told that we are only human,
that we are not meant for greatness,
that we are meant to suffer and endure,
and that we are not meant to be saved.

But what if I am tired? What if I am weak?
What if I cannot bear the weight of this burden?
What if I am not strong enough, not brave enough,
Not resilient enough to carry on?

What if I want to cry, to scream, to give up?
What if I am only human, with all my flaws and faults,
with all my doubts and fears, with all my imperfections?
What if I want to be saved, to be held, to be loved?

But the world does not care. It demands, it expects,
it takes and takes and takes, without giving anything
back.
It tells us to be perfect, to be invincible,

to be superhuman, when we are only human.

And so we carry on, with the weight of this burden,
this burden of being human, heavy on our shoulders.
But sometimes, in the quiet moments, when no one is
watching,
we allow ourselves to be weak, to be vulnerable, to be
human.

20. Swimming Lessons

I am learning to swim in the ocean of my mistakes,
Drowning in the weight of my wrongs, trying to stay
afloat.

I am gasping for air, struggling to find my way,
But the waves keep crashing over me, pulling me down.

I am trying to swim against the tide of my past,
But the current is so strong that I am swept away.

I am sinking deeper and deeper into the darkness,
Fighting against the memories that haunt me.

But I am determined to keep going, to keep trying,
To not let my mistakes swallow me whole.

I am learning to be a better version of myself,
To rise above the chaos of my past.

I am finding my strength, my resilience,
In this ocean of mistakes, I am learning to swim.

21. My Own Hero

Why must I look at others for inspiration?
Why must I cling to their every word
like a beggar out in the cold?

I'm a strong person
and I will be my own hero.

My words are powerful
and I will use them to inspire myself.

My heart is strong
and I will use this to stay true to me.

I am a hero in my own right,
a warrior, a poet, a force to be reckoned with.

I will stand tall and face my fears,
I will speak my mind and hold my ground.

I don't need someone else to rescue me,
I can save myself from the darkness within.

I am a fighter,
strong and fierce and unbreakable.

I am my own hero,
and I will never let myself down.

For I have the power within,
to conquer any challenge that comes my way.

I am my own hero,
and I will pave my own path.

No longer will I look to others for strength,
for I have found it within myself.

I am my own hero,
and I will rise above any obstacle.

So let me be an inspiration to others,
a reminder that they, too, have the power within.

For I am my own hero,
and I will continue to shine bright.

I may falter.
I may stumble.
I may fall.

I will be my own hero, and pick myself up.